A Note to Parents

Dorling Kindersley Readers is a compelling new program for beginning readers, designed in conjunction with leading literacy experts, including Dr. Linda Gambrell, Director of the School of Education at Clemson University. Dr. Gambrell has served on the Board of Directors of the International Reading Association and as President of the National Reading Conference.

Beautiful illustrations and superb full-color photographs combine with engaging, easy-to-read stories to offer a fresh approach to each subject in the series. Each *Dorling Kindersley Reader* is guaranteed to capture a child's interest while developing his or her reading skills, general knowledge, and love of reading.

The four levels of *Dorling Kindersley Readers* are aimed at different reading abilities, enabling you to choose the books that are exactly right for your child:

Level 1 – Beginning to read
Level 2 – Beginning to read alone
Level 3 – Reading alone
Level 4 – Proficient readers

The "normal" age at which a child begins to read can be anywhere from three to eight years old, so these levels are intended only as a general guideline.

No matter which level you select, you can be sure that you are helping your child learn to read, then read to learn!

Dorling **DK** Kindersley

LONDON, NEW YORK, SYDNEY, DELHI, PARIS,
MUNICH, and JOHANNESBURG

Project Editor Caroline Bingham
Art Editor Helen Melville

For Dorling Kindersley
Managing Editor Bridget Gibbs
Senior Art Editor Clare Shedden
Senior DTP Designer Bridget Roseberry
US Editor Adrienne Betz
Production Shivani Pandey
Picture Researcher Marie Osborn
Jacket Designer Yumiko Tahata
Indexer Lynn Bresler
Illustrator Malcolm Chandler

Reading Consultant
Linda Gambrell, Ph.D.

First American Edition, 2001
00 01 02 03 04 05 10 9 8 7 6 5 4 3 2 1
Published in the United States by DK Publishing, Inc.
95 Madison Avenue, New York, New York 10016

Published in Great Britain by Dorling Kindersley Limited.

Library of Congress Catalog #.
LCCN 00-055525

ISBN 0-7894-7381-X (pbk) ISBN 0-7894-7382-8 (hc)

The publisher would like to thank the following for their kind permission
to reproduce their images:
Key: c=center; b=bottom; l=left; r=right' t=top
AKG London: 7, 33; **Bridgeman Art Library,** London/New York: 32, 49;
Crown Estate/Institute of Directors, London: 9; **Johnny Van Haeften Ltd,**
London: 10-11, 48; **Mary Evans Picture Library:** 21, 22b; **Greenpeace
Inc:** Mer Jenburgh 38; **Illustrated London News Picture Library:** 14b, 15,
26-27; **Peter Newark's Pictures:** 2, 3, 6, 35, 36-37; **Stanley L. Wood:** 8;
NASA: 7tr; **Naval Historical Center:** 23, 28; **National Maritime
Museum:** 20; **Rex Features:** Sipa 44, 45tl, 45tr; **The Stock Market:** 12;
Tony Stone Images: Christian Lagereek 46-47; **Topham Picturepoint:**
39cr, 43; **TRH Pictures:** 30-31; **Imperial War Museum:** 34.
Jacket: **Corbis:** front; **National Maritime Museum:** back.

Color reproduction by Colourscan, Singapore
Printed and bound by L. Rex Printing Co. Ltd

see our complete
catalog at
www.dk.com

Contents

DK DORLING KINDERSLEY *READERS*

READING
3
ALONE

DISASTERS
AT SEA

Written by Andrew Donkin

A Dorling Kindersley Book

"Abandon ship!"

The oceans of the world can be dangerous, even for experienced sailors.

Hidden rocks and coral reefs can tear holes in a ship's hull. Powerful storms and hurricanes can damage ships or rip them apart.

1989: The Exxon Valdez's *huge oil spill spreads pollution along 1,000 miles of the Alaskan coastline.*

1854: The passenger liner, the Arctic, *is traveling through fog when another ship suddenly appears on a collision course!*

1879: The brave crew of the Jeannette *set out to reach the North Pole!*

Thick fog can increase the chances of a collision with another ship, with the coastline, or with an iceberg. Finally, people make mistakes. Human error can turn even the safest ship into just one more shipwreck on the ocean floor.

This book tells the stories of some of the worst disasters that ever happened on the ocean's waves.

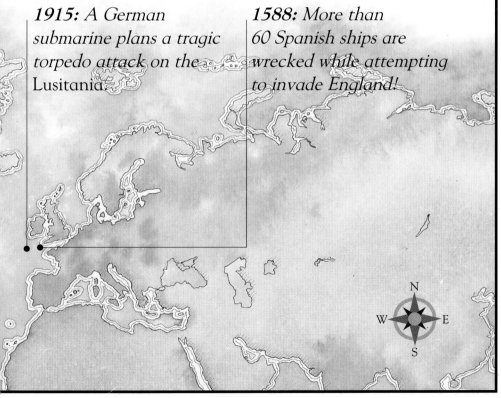

1915: A German submarine plans a tragic torpedo attack on the Lusitania.

1588: More than 60 Spanish ships are wrecked while attempting to invade England!

Invasion!

King Philip II

King Philip II of Spain was looking forward to a glorious victory.

"We have waited a long time to invade England," he proclaimed. "The Armada will help us to do it."

The Armada was made up of 132 warships, with 20,000 Spanish soldiers on board. The King believed that it was the greatest war fleet in history. He called it his invincible Armada because he was sure that no one could defeat it.

The Armada set sail for Britain, keeping in a tight battle formation.

Under the command of Lord Howard and Sir Francis Drake, the British fleet was ready for the Armada. The British fleet was much smaller, but they had some advantages.

"I know the way the Spanish like
to fight," insisted Drake. "They'll try
to get close enough to board our ships
so that their soldiers can engage us in
hand-to-hand combat. We must keep
our distance and use our cannons!"

The two fleets played a cat-and-
mouse game for days, with a few small
battles. It soon became obvious that the
British ships were easier to maneuver
than the huge Spanish galleons.
The British moved fast. Boom! Their
cannon fire devastated the Spanish
vessels. Then they made a quick getaway!

Gunpowder

Gunpowder was the first explosive to be invented. It is made from a mixture of sulphur, charcoal, and a chemical called saltpetre.

Having suffered the worst of several battles, the Armada anchored near the French coast to collect fresh supplies and more ammunition. At midnight, the British launched a new attack!

Eight British ships were packed with gunpowder and sailed straight at the Spanish. At the last moment, sailors lit the gunpowder and escaped in rowboats. Panic and confusion spread through the Spanish ranks as they tried to avoid the deadly fireships.

The next day's vicious fighting lasted eight hours. The scattered Armada suffered terrible damage.

Medina Sidonia, the Armada's once proud Commander-in-Chief, knew that now there was only one thing to do. "We must retreat," he said.

To avoid the English fleet, Sidonia chose to sail home around the north of Scotland. It would prove to be a mistake. Fierce storms blew ship after ship on to the rocks of the Scottish and Irish coasts.

Food and water ran out. Each sailor had only a few biscuits to eat each day.

When the remains of the Armada finally returned to Spain it was a sorry sight. A total of 63 ships had been lost and 11,000 men had died. The invasion of England had been a disaster.

Full steam ahead!

 Date: *1854*
Place: *North Atlantic ocean*

Captain Luce was in a hurry. He was in command of the *Arctic*, one of the fastest passenger ships on the ocean. The vessel had sailed from England, heading homewards towards New York.

About 60 miles from the American coast, the *Arctic* moved into an area of thick gray fog.

"Keep her at full speed," ordered Captain Luce.

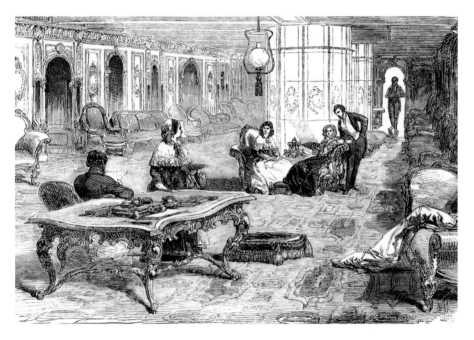

The steamer's powerful paddles churned up the sea water as they pushed her on towards port. Some passengers were eating lunch while others were relaxing below decks. But all was not well.

A dark metallic shape suddenly loomed out of the fog. It was heading straight towards the *Arctic*!

"It's another ship! Change course!" ordered the Captain, but it was too late.

The *Vesta*, a smaller French vessel, rammed straight into the *Arctic*'s side. There was a horrible sound of metal being stretched and then ripped apart.

The *Arctic*'s passengers and crew were sent tumbling to the floor.

The two captains inspected the damage to their ships.

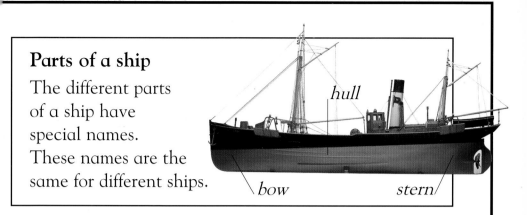

Parts of a ship

The different parts
of a ship have
special names.
These names are the
same for different ships.

hull

bow

stern

They saw that the bigger vessel, the *Arctic*, had a hole in its hull. The *Vesta* had ten feet of her bow area missing!

The *Vesta* was taking on water quickly. It didn't look as if she would stay afloat for long. Captain Luce decided that he could not risk the *Arctic* and his own passengers' safety to stop and help.

"Set a course straight for the nearest port!" he ordered.

The *Vesta*'s crew and passengers watched in horror as the *Arctic* turned and sailed away, abandoning them to their fate!

The commander of the *Vesta*, Captain Duchesne, had to think quickly.

"Lighten the ship!" he ordered. "Throw the cargo and anything else you can move into the sea!"

The crew rushed around, grabbing everything they could lift and throwing it overboard.

Amazingly the ship's bow began to lift out of the water. The *Vesta* was saved.

Several days later, the *Vesta* limped slowly into port. Captain Duchesne was still angry. Where was the *Arctic*, the ship that had deserted him? To his surprise, he was told that the *Arctic* had never made it back!

What had happened to the *Arctic*?

The ship had been more heavily damaged than anyone had first thought. She had three holes – not just one – in her hull. One hole was as wide as a car and sea water kept rushing in!

As the ship headed toward shore, the crew had kept pumping out water. But after four hours, the rising waters had flooded the engine room.

Captain Luce knew there was no hope left. He gave the order to abandon ship! But there were not enough lifeboats and people panicked, fighting for a place.

Lifeboats

In an emergency, lifeboats are winched over the side of a ship to allow everyone to escape.

Out of the 435 people on board, only 85 survived. One of the survivors was Captain Luce, who spent two days clinging to wreckage before being rescued. Too late, he realized that if he had stayed to help the *Vesta*, the French ship could probably have saved them all.

Ice trap!

Date: *July 8, 1879*
Place: *San Francisco, west coast of America*

The crowd on the San Francisco shoreline began to cheer as they saw that the ship was finally hoisting its anchor. The well-wishers had gathered to wave off the *Jeannette*, a 420-ton coal-burning steamer.

The reason for the great excitement was that the ship was leaving on a very special mission. Her commander, Lieutenant George De Long, was

Lieutenant George De Long

determined to lead the first expedition to reach the North Pole!

At the end of the nineteenth century, reaching the North Pole was one of the last explorations still to be made. Many people believed that an ice-free route existed all the way.

De Long was confident that he and his ship would find this route and become famous. He ordered his men to set course for the Arctic Ocean.

Coal

Coal is a black mineral which is found underground. It is the remains of fossilized trees which are millions of years old. Coal is burned to provide power.

The crew and scientists on board the *Jeannette* were in high spirits as the ship entered the colder waters around Alaska. In mid-August, they stopped to take on fresh food and more coal, then headed north once more looking for a route that would lead them to the Pole.

"My heart is set on this expedition and her success," wrote De Long in his daily journal.

The ship continued to make good progress. Loose fragments of ice littered the waterways, but the powerful steamer plowed through them.

De Long kept hoping that his ship would sail all the way to the Pole. He began to doubt this as the ship headed deeper into the icefield. The ice was getting thicker and thicker.

"We can't go forward any more, sir. It's solid pack ice!" reported the second mate. He sounded anxious.

The ship headed northwest instead. The crew hoped to find openings that might lead through the icy mass.

Everybody was starting to worry that the ship might get stuck.

By September 6, the ice was refreezing around the ship as quickly as she could break it. It was no use.

"We're trapped, sir!" cried a crew member.

The *Jeannette* had twisted and turned to navigate 60 miles into the icefield. Now she was stuck until warmer weather melted the ice.

Around the ship, the ice sheets moved closer, grinding and crushing against one another.

As the weeks turned to months, the icefield around the *Jeannette* did not melt. But worse was yet to come.

The ship strained as huge slabs of ice shifted and pushed against the port (left-hand) side. From inside the *Jeannette* came the sound of snapping timbers and twisting metal.

"She's being squeezed to death!"

The men escaped onto the ice just moments before the crushed ship disappeared beneath the surface.

The *Jeannette* expedition had learned the hard way that there was no ice-free route to the Pole. They were alone on an icepack. The men faced a journey of hundreds of miles across an icy wasteland to reach safety.

Tragically, of the 33 men who set out on the *Jeannette* full of hope, ambition, and wonder, only 13 returned.

Direct hit!

"The extra lookouts are in place, sir," reported the First Officer.

"Excellent. Make sure they're alert and that each man takes a regular break," ordered Captain Turner.

Captain Turner was in command of the *Lusitania*, a magnificent British ocean liner more than 760 feet long! In his care were nearly 2,000 passengers and crew members.

The *Lusitania* was nearing the end of a trip from America to England. What made this voyage particularly dangerous was that England and Germany were at war – World War I had begun. Germany had just announced that it would send its submarines, called U-boats, to sink British ships!

Captain Turner wanted to make sure that his ship avoided danger but he was already too late.

Periscope

This is a long tube with mirrors at both ends. It lets people in a submarine see what is happening above the surface of the sea.

Staring through his periscope, the commander of U-boat *U-20* watched the huge bulk of the *Lusitania* steam towards him. Captain Walter Schweiger had spotted the passenger liner as soon as her smoke stacks had first appeared over the horizon.

"Stand by!" ordered the German captain.

U-20 had already sunk several ships, but the *Lusitania* would easily be the most important. However, Captain Schweiger suddenly began to wonder if they had enough torpedoes left.

It would probably take two or even three torpedoes to sink a ship that size.

He waited patiently until the *Lusitania* was just 2,000 feet away.

"Fire!"

A single torpedo smashed into the *Lusitania*'s starboard (right-hand) side. A loud explosion shook the entire ship.

"U-boat!" screamed a crew member.

Seawater rushed into the *Lusitania*'s damaged hull. The weight of the water made the ship lean steeply to one side.

From the safety of his U-boat, the German Captain watched thick black smoke streaming from the ship. Would he need to use another torpedo?

Boom! Without warning there was another explosion aboard the *Lusitania*!

Torpedo

A large, cigar-shaped weapon packed with explosives. It is fired by a submarine or ship and is aimed at enemy shipping.

The ship was carrying ammunition as part of its cargo and the German torpedo had made it explode.

The explosion had done just as good a job of finishing the *Lusitania* as a second torpedo. The ship was sinking fast.

Passengers and crew rushed onto the deck. Everyone was trying to get into a lifeboat. The damage and the crowding of people on the deck caused the ship to tilt or list. As the list became worse, the ropes used to lower the lifeboats jammed and tangled. The job of launching the little lifeboats was now almost impossible.

Time had run out for the ship. It took less than 20 minutes for it to sink.

Only 6 of the *Lusitania*'s 48 lifeboats made it to shore, even though the coast was just a few miles away. The torpedo's unlucky strike cost 1,195 people their lives.

Spill!

 Date: *March 24, 1989*
Place: *Alaska*

The gigantic ship moved slowly underneath the clear night sky. The *Exxon Valdez* weighed more than 200,000 tons, and was 987 feet long. It had just left Valdez in Alaska carrying a huge cargo of crude oil to California.

Crude oil
This is a thick black fluid that is found underground. It can be refined, which changes it into gasoline for running car engines.

The massive vessel, known as a VLCC or Very Large Crude Carrier, had a crew of 20. She was under the command of Captain Joseph Hazelwood, an experienced sea voyager.

Captain Joseph Hazelwood

"Captain, there are some growlers ahead!" warned the officer on watch.

Growlers are small icebergs. They weren't large enough to sink the *Exxon Valdez*, but they could dent her hull.

"Radio the coastguard," ordered Captain Hazelwood.

The *Exxon Valdez* was given permission to change shipping lanes and go around the icebergs.

Ahead now lay the dangerous task of steering the huge ship through the narrow seaway between Busby Island and Bligh Reef. Bligh Reef is covered with jagged rocks and it is a dangerous place for ships. Yet the Captain chose this moment to hand over command to the ship's third mate, Greg Cousins.

"I'll be in my cabin if you need me," said the Captain as he left the bridge.

The ship sailed on through the cold night. Just after midnight, Cousins saw that they were getting too close to Bligh Reef and ordered a small course change. He began to plot the new course but when he checked again two minutes later, he saw to his horror that his order hadn't been properly obeyed.

The ship was now directly over the sharp rocks of Bligh Reef!

Cousins tried to contact Captain Hazelwood. Even as he did so, a terrible shudder ripped through the ship.

"Rocks!"

The rocks were only 50 feet below the surface of the water, but the ship's hull went deeper than this. The ship had run aground.

As the ship continued forward, the rocks tore open 11 giant cargo tanks full of crude oil. The sticky black liquid began to gush out of the *Exxon Valdez*'s hull.

The crew members were powerless. All they could do was radio for help.

As the tide dropped during the next few hours, more than 11 million gallons of thick crude oil leaked from the ship into the sea.

An emergency clean-up operation gradually got underway. Another smaller tanker was positioned next to the trapped *Exxon Valdez* so that its remaining oil could be pumped out.

An army of workers began the painfully slow job of removing oil from the surface of the ocean with special tools called booms and skimmers.

Nearly 50,000 workers were used in the operation. It was a difficult task because wildlife in the area had already begun to die.

Preparation of booms for use in the Exxon Valdez *clean-up operation.*

Thick sticky crude oil was washed ashore along 1,000 miles of Alaska's once beautiful coastline. The oil stuck to birds' feathers and it poisoned fish and other sea life.

Casualties of the oil slick included whales, sea otters, and many kinds of fish. Some seabirds were caught and cleaned by hand, but for half a million birds it was too late. The oil had caused a massive environmental disaster.

"Mayday! Mayday!"

The seas of the world are still dangerous, although today they are probably safer than they have ever been.

Most modern ships are fitted with both radar, which lets sailors see what is ahead of them in the dark or in thick fog, and also echolocation devices, which let the crew "see" what is below the ship.

Global positioning satellites (GPS) circling high above the Earth send down signals. These signals allow modern ships to pinpoint their exact position anywhere in the world. Other satellites

Global positioning satellite

provide information about the weather so that ships can avoid storms and high winds which may lie ahead.

Sadly, despite the technology sailors now have, there will always be some disasters at sea. That's because there will always be people in charge, and people make mistakes.

Glossary

Ammunition
Any kind of bullets, cannon shells or other explosives that are fired from a weapon.

Bow
The front section of a ship.

Echolocation
A way of finding things by measuring how long it takes for sound waves to bounce off them.

Fleet
A number or group of ships all from the same navy or the same country.

Galleon
A large sailing ship with tall masts. It is usually Spanish.

Hull
The frame of a ship.

Hurricane
A powerful tropical storm, which can cause massive destruction.

Icefield
An area where icebergs are very common.

Lieutenant
An officer in the navy.

Navigate
To control the direction and course of a ship.

Pack ice
Dangerous areas where the sea has frozen to form large masses of floating ice. Pack ice can crush a ship.

Port
The left-hand side of a ship.

Radar
A way of using radio waves to "see" what is ahead of a ship in the dark or in fog. Or a device that picks up the radio waves.

Satellite
A device that orbits Earth and sends down useful information from space.

Shipping lane
A route on an ocean or sea that is used regularly by many ships.

Shipwreck
The sinking or destruction of a ship by a storm, by running onto rocks, by a collision, or by enemy attack.

Starboard
The right-hand side of a ship.

Steamer
A ship powered by large stream-driven engines.

Stern
The rear (back) section of a ship

Technology
The latest and most advanced scientific equipment.